Col. 2:3
In whom are
hid all the
treasures

of wisdom
and
knowledge

SEEKING & FINDING
GOD'S
HIDDEN
TREASURE

*by **Cherilyn Buhlmann***

Book design Copyright © 2018.   All rights reserved.

RWG Publishing
PO Box 596
Litchfield, IL 62056
https://rwgpublishing.com/

Published in the United States of America

Paperback: 978-1791555283

Contents

ACKNOWLEDGMENTS FROM CHERILYN BUHLMANN

I give my Heavenly Father all the glory and praise for leading me in my seeking to know Him more. Through the blessing of holding devotions with my co-workers at Southeastern University in Lakeland, Florida, God has given me insight in His Word I count as treasures. They are hidden treasures, as God's Word so says until they are found. Jesus is 'the find' of a lifetime...

the *everlasting kind.* He brings a glimmer of light to the glass the Word says, we see through darkly, as we seek the things of God.

I thank God for the support I have received from my husband, Rudolf Buhlmann, my parents, Carlyn and Josephine Kulick for our family's Christian heritage, my Pastors Stephen and Jan Strader of Ignited Church in Lakeland for their unrelenting passion to lead us to be passionate to God. *Ann* Kiemel, who inspired me through her stories and singing a little song, in the 70's. She shared the love of Jesus one person at a time, and exclaimed, "Jesus and me are out to change the world." And they did.

6

I thank God for my life line: my three children, Angel, Jeremy, Abraham and three grandchildren, Shelby, Bailey and Channing.

I pray that you find these devotions a treasure to your heart also and that you *seek* and *find* for yourself how awesome our God really is.

Mysteries Hidden and Revealed

Romans 16:25 "According to the revelation of the mystery which was kept secret since the world began."

Matthew 13:11,16,17 Jesus said, "It is given unto you to know the mysteries of the kingdom of heaven. Blessed are your eyes, for they *see:* and your ears, for they hear. For verily I say unto you, that many prophets and righteous men have desired to *see* those things which ye see, and have not seen them, and to hear those things which ye hear, and have not heard them."

I Peter 1:10-12 "Of which salvation the prophets have inquired and searched diligently, who prophesied of the grace that should come unto you. Unto whom it was revealed that not unto themselves, but unto us they did minister the things which are now reported unto you by them that have preached the gospel; which things the angels desire to look into."

Ephesians 3:5,6 "Which in other ages, was not made known unto the sons of men, *as* it is now revealed *that the gentiles should be fellow heirs, and of the same body and partakers of His promise in Christ by the gospel."*

Revelation is, a covering taken off and the mystery removed, so that all can *see.* Oh, the mystery of that day, when Jesus' Bride, the Church will have her covering and veil removed so that all can *see* who the beautiful Church is. We are a mystery - let's not keep it a *secret!*

The Ultimate Planner

Jeremiah 29:11 "For I know the plans that I have for you" declares the Lord, "plans for well-being, and not for calamity, in order to give you a future and a hope." (ISV)

Jeremiah 29:12-14 "Then shall ye call upon Me, and ye shall go and pray unto Me, and I will hearken unto you. And ye shall *seek* Me, and find Me, when ye shall search for Me with all your heart. And I will be found of you, saith the Lord."

In that day the heavenly invitation was given to the shepherds to *"find* the babe wrapped in swaddling clothes, lying in a manger." Luke 2:12

"The shepherds said one to another, let us now *go* even unto Bethlehem, and *see* this thing which is come to pass, which the Lord hath made known unto us. And they came with haste and *found* Mary and Joseph, and the babe lying in a manger. And when they had seen it, they made known abroad the saying which was told them concerning this child." Luke 2:15-17

When the days of Mary's purification was accomplished, they brought Him to Jerusalem to present Him to the Lord and to offer sacrifice.

Luke 2:25-33 "And behold, there was a man in Jerusalem, whose name was Simeon; and the same man was just and devout, waiting for the consolation of Israel, and the Holy Ghost was upon him.

And it was revealed unto him by the Holy Ghost, that he should not see death, before he had seen the Lord's Christ. And he came by the Spirit into the temple: and when the parents brought in the child Jesus, to do for Him after the custom of the law, then took he Him up in his arms, and blessed God, and said, Lord, now lettest thou thy servant depart in peace, according to Thy word; for mine eyes have seen Thy salvation, which Thou hast prepared before the face of all people; *A Light to lighten the Gentiles, and the glory of Thy people, Israel,* and Joseph and his mother marveled at those things which were spoken of Him."

This first announcement by a Jewish prophet proclaims that Jesus was to be a light to the Gentiles. It took a divine, rebuke for the apostles to concede such a doctrine. It was over this, that controversies raged in the early church. (Acts 10:18 and 11:18)

(Acts 15, Gal. 2) This was the mystery that was kept *secret* from the foundation of the world and it came from Simeon's lips, that the Gentiles would be shown this Light and should be fellow heirs in Christ.

Christmas is Something Else!

Christmas is celebrated with the knowledge that angels brought *"good tidings,"* *peace* is pronounced and declared, and *salvation* is God's gift to mankind through the birth of His Son, Jesus.

When we celebrate Christmas, we get a taste, a preview and a glimpse of the future of God's Millennial reign! In that day, all men on earth will see face to face the Lord and resurrected saints of all ages. Watchmen who in times past had alerted the people when enemies approached, will in that day, rejoice seeing the remnant of Israel returning to Jerusalem to make the Millennial nation.

Isaiah 52:7-9 "How beautiful upon the mountains are the feet of Him that bringeth *good tidings,* that publisheth *peace,* that bringeth good tidings of good, that publisheth *salvation;* that saith unto Zion, thy God reigneth! Thy watchmen shall lift up the voice; with the voice together shall they sing; for they shall see eye to eye, when the Lord shall bring again Zion. Break forth into joy, sing together, ye waste places of Jerusalem: for the Lord hath comforted His people, He hath redeemed Jerusalem."

As Jesus has said, "this do in remembrance of Me." Have a blessed Christmas remembering what Christ has done for us and will do in our future.

Assignment 2012: come to Order

We have entered the year 2012. What do these numbers mean to you? Twenty is expectation. Twelve is God's Divine Power, Rule and Authority. As we prepare ourselves for this year, let us align ourselves to the position where God can unfold His Sovereign plan in each of us. God wants us to bring it to order: our lives, church body, community, region, leaders, country and the whole earth to Come to Order. Let us declare it, decree it and cause it to happen; as raising and sounding of a Judges Gavel - Bring it to Order!

Romans 12:1 " I beseech you therefore, brethren, by the mercies of God, that ye present your bodies a living sacrifice, holy, acceptable unto God, *which is* your reasonable service."

Leviticus 1:7-8 As the burnt offering was offered unto the Lord... "lay the wood in *order* upon the fire... lay the parts, the head of the fat, *in order* upon the wood that is on the fire which is upon the Altar." May *we* also lay our lives *in order* before God.

There are many instances showing God's divine authority through the number twelve. Twelve hours a day, to the night, twelve months to the year, and twelve constellations. In the New Jerusalem, twelve gates, pearls, twelve kinds of precious stones representing the twelve Apostles. Twelve manner of fruit on the tree of Life and bore its fruit every month of the twelve months. Twelve is also very pertinent in the measuring of making the Tabernacle.

Be excited for this year! Let us proclaim:

"Let Your Kingdom come, Let Your will be done, let us *see the Glory* of Your Son."

It's 'the Relationship!'

Tomorrow *is* Valentine's Day. Romantics favor the tale of the third-century roman physician and priest Valentine. He secretly had married couples in the military - against the Kings orders. Supposedly, he had fallen in love with the jailer's daughter and shortly before the day of his execution, he wrote to her on a card "with all my love, your Valentine."

Romans 8:35,38,39 "Who shall separate us from the love of Christ? For I am persuaded, that neither death, nor life, nor angels, nor principalities, nor powers, nor things present, nor things to come, nor height, nor depth, nor any other creature, shall be able to separate us from the love of God, which is in Christ Jesus our Lord."

I met a young man who shared with me that he was confused with finding which religion is the right choice. Deep in my spirit I knew only one answer to tell him, "This book on religions you're reading is only statistics. It's not the religion, *it's the Relationship!"* He said how could this happen, that we met up at this place and time?" It was a God appointment.

Whether were celebrating Valentines with someone special or feeling the love of our heavenly Father...

It's in 'the Relationship!'

Love of God, over flow, permeate all my soul!

Minister to Jesus

On this earth Jesus ministered to many people, feeding thousands and healing the sick. We know that he spent much time in prayer with his Father. Jesus would often route His journeys to allow a stopover at a home in Bethany, which belonged to His cousins, Lazarus, Mary, and Martha. This was a treasured place in this world because it was there that *He was ministered to by others.* It was the blessed dwelling where Mary sat at His feet and absorbed His every word and had poured her much priced Alabaster Jar of perfume over His feet.

Imagine Jesus speaking to the multitudes of people in the various places He would go, yet they were there to *hear* what He had to say. In the Bethany home, *He felt the love as* we feel *when we come together* at our places of worship. I'd like to believe they had the first experience of having church, and *Jesus was there.*

John 12:1-3 "Then Jesus six days before the passover, came to Bethany where Lazarus was which had been dead, whom He raised from the dead. There they made Him a supper; and Martha served: but Lazarus was one of them that sat at the table with him. Then took Mary a pound of ointment of spikenard, very costly, and anointed the feet of

Jesus, and wiped His feet with her hair: and the house was filled with the odor of the ointment."

They saw Jesus the man, whole heartedly receive their encouragement as *they ministered to Him.* When we minister to others, *we are doing it as unto Him.*

Matthew 25:37,40 "Then shall the righteous answer Him, saying, Lord, when saw we Thee an hungred, and fed *Thee?* or thirsty, and gave *Thee* drink? And the King shall answer and say unto them, Verily I say unto you, Inasmuch as ye have done *it* unto one of the least of these my brethren, <u>ye have done *it* unto Me.</u>"

I Call you Friends

Romans 8:28b "to them who are the called according to *His* purpose."

Mark 3:13-15 " And He goeth up into a mountain, and calleth unto Him whom He would: and they came unto Him. And He ordained twelve, that they should be with Him, and that He might send them forth to preach, and to have power to heal sicknesses, and to cast out devils."

Of the twelve, there was an inner circle of three who were closer to Jesus than the rest. They were Simon Peter, James, and John. Jesus seemed to confide in them more, allowing them to share in His pain at the Garden of Gethsemane, and His glory at the Mount of Transfiguration on a unique level.

John 15:15 " Henceforth I call you not servants; for the servant knoweth not what his Lord doeth: but *I have called you friends;* for all things that I have heard of my Father I have made known unto you."

John was the closest friend to Jesus. He sat next to Jesus at the Last Supper, he alone stood by Jesus at the *Cross,* and on Resurrection morning - his passion caused him to out run even Peter to the empty tomb!

Let John's persuaded way of living bring us to a place to become a friend of God. Let's not be among the crowd or at a distance, but *with* Him at the foot of the Cross.

To be a good friend to others:

F have good *fellowship*

R be *reliable*

I be an *inspiration*

E be an *encourager*

N be *neighborly*

D be a *disciple*

And what avails us when we call on the name of the Lord?

Acts 2:21 ..."whosoever shall *call on* the name of the Lord *shall be saved!"*

THE LAMB OF GOD - KING OF KINGS AND LORD OF LORDS

Philippians 2:5-8 "Let this mind be in you, which was also in Christ Jesus: Who, being in the form of God, thought it not robbery to be equal with God: But made himself of no reputation, and took upon Him the form of a servant, and was made in the likeness of men: And being found in fashion as a man, He humbled himself, and became obedient unto death, even the death of the cross."

Isaiah 53:3-7,9a "He is despised and rejected of men; a man of sorrows, and acquainted with grief: and we hid as it were *our* faces from Him; He was despised and we esteemed Him not. Surely He hath borne our griefs, and carried our sorrows: yet we did esteem Him stricken, smitten of God, and afflicted. But He *was* wounded for our transgressions, He *was* bruised for our iniquities: the chastisement of our peace *was* upon Him; and with His stripes we are healed. All we like sheep have gone astray; we have turned every one to his own way; and the LORD hath laid on Him the iniquity of us all. He was oppressed, and He was afflicted, yet He opened not His mouth: He is brought as a lamb to the slaughter, and as a sheep before her shearers is dumb, so He openeth not His mouth. And He made His grave with the wicked, and with the rich in His death;"

Matthew 27:51-54 "And, behold, the veil of the temple was rent in twain from the top to the bottom; and the earth did quake, and the rocks rent; And the graves were opened; and many bodies of the saints which slept arose, And came out of the graves <u>after His resurrection,</u> and went into the holy city, and appeared unto many.

Now when the centurion, and they that were with him watching Jesus, saw the earthquake, and those things that were done, they feared greatly, saying, truly this was the Son of God.

Matthew 28:1-9 " In the end of the sabbath, as it began to dawn toward the first day of the week, came Mary Magdalene and the other Mary to see the sepulchre. And, behold, there was a great earthquake: for the angel of the Lord descended from heaven, and came and rolled back the stone from the door, and sat upon it. His countenance was like lightning, and his rament white as snow: And for fear of him the keepers did shake, and became as dead *men.*

And the angel answered and said unto the women, Fear not ye: for I know that ye seek Jesus, which was crucified. He is not here: for He is risen, as He said. Come, see the place where the Lord lay.

And go quickly, and tell His disciples that He is risen from the dead; and, behold, He goeth before you into Galilee; there shall ye *see* Him: lo, I have told you. And they departed quickly from the sepulchre with fear and great joy; and did run to bring His disciples word.

And as they went to tell His disciples, behold, Jesus met them, saying, 'All hail.' And they came and held Him by the feet, and worshipped Him.

Praise the Lord! We are redeemed. Let the redeemed of the Lord say so!

Clean before the Lord I stand, and in me not one blemish does He see. When I place my burdens on Him, He takes them all, from me. (song)

ON THE WAY TO EMMAUS

On the day Jesus had risen from the dead:

Luke 24:13-32 "And, behold, two of them went that same day to a village called Emmaus, which was from Jerusalem about threescore furlongs. And they talked together of all these things which had happened. And it came to pass, that while they *communed together* and reasoned, Jesus himself drew near, and went with them. But their eyes were *holden* that they should not know Him. And He said unto them, What manner of communications *are* these that ye have one to another, as ye walk and are sad? And the one of them whose name was Cleopas, answering said unto Him, Art thou only a stranger in Jerusalem, and hast not known the things which are come to pass there in these days? And He said unto them, What things? And they said unto Him, concerning *Jesus* of Nazareth, which was a prophet mighty in deed and word before God and all the people: And how the chief priests and our rulers delivered Him to be condemned to death, and have crucified Him. But we trusted that it had been He which should have redeemed Israel: and beside all this, today is the third day since these things were done.

Yea, and certain women also of our company made us astonished, which were early at the sepulchre; And when they found not His body, they came, saying, that they had also seen a vision of angels, which said that He was alive.

And certain of them which were with us went to the sepulchre, and found *it* even so as the women had said: but Him they saw not.

Then He said unto them, 0 fools, and slow of heart to believe all that the prophets have spoken:

Ought not Christ to have suffered these things, and to enter into his glory?

And beginning at Moses and all the prophets, *He expounded unto them in all the scriptures the things concerning Himself.* And they drew nigh unto the village, whither they went: and He made as though He would have gone further. But they constrained Him, saying, *abide* with us: for it is toward evening, and the day is far spent. And He went in to tarry with them. And it came to pass, as He sat at meat with them, He took bread, and blessed *it,* and brake, and gave to them. And *their eyes were opened,* and they *knew* Him; and He vanished out of their sight. And they said one to another, Did not *our heart burn within us,* while He talked with us by the way, and while He opened to us the scriptures?"

Before Jesus appeared on the scene the two men *communed together.* A form of the word communion. Jesus asks us to, "Do this in remembrance of Me." As Jesus broke bread and gave to them, their *eyes were opened* to what He wanted them to *see.* Let us desire to *see of God* when we partake in communion, and may our hearts burn within us, also.

Know your Calling

What one situation has changed your life? Oral Roberts held a tent revival service in the beginning of his ministry. As he was speaking forth his message to the people, a man shot at him. The bullet whizzed by his head and went through the back of the tent. This story spread like wild fire and the world came to know of the unknown minister from Oklahoma. Most likely, what happened that day caused him to understand the hope of his calling.

Ephesians 1:18-19 "The eyes of your understanding being enlightened; that ye may know what is the hope of his calling, and what the riches of the glory of his inheritance in the saints. And what is the exceeding greatness of His power to us-ward who believe, according to the working of His mighty power."

Know your calling - know in your knower. Do it with excellence and might.

Isaiah 58:8,11 "Then shall thy light break forth as the morning, and thine health shall spring forth speedily: and thy righteousness shall go before thee: the glory of the Lord shall be your rear guard. And the Lord shall guide thee continually, and satisfy thy soul in drought, and make fat thy bones: and thou shalt be like a watered garden, and like a spring of water, whose waters fail not."

Be filled to overflowing. It is a custom in the Middle East, when guests finish a meal in one's home, they are served a drink just before they leave. Upon how much is in each ones glass, that determines if they are welcome to come again. If the drink is full to overflowing, the host is eager to have their company again. I wonder how very little drink there would be, if the guest would not be welcomed there again.

More importantly, we would want to know the Lord is pleased with our communion with Him - and assuredly, He is always eager to have our company again.

So let us be constantly renewed in the Spirit of our mind, have a fresh mental and spiritual attitude, and put on the new nature as we were created to be.

He will fill your heart today to overflowing, *As* the Lord commandeth you;

bring your *vessels,* not a few.

He will fill your heart today to overflowing, with the Holy Ghost and power.   (song)

Ezekiel's River

Ezekiel 47:1-5 "Afterward he brought me again unto the door of the house; and, behold, waters issued out from under the threshold of the house eastward: for the forefront of the house *stood toward* the east, and the waters came down from under from the right side of the house, at the south *side* of the altar. Then brought he me out of the way of the gate northward, and led me about the way without unto the utter gate by the way that looketh eastward; and, behold, there ran out waters on the right side. And when the man that had the line in his hand went forth eastward, he measured a thousand cubits, and he brought me through the waters; the waters *were* to the ankles. Again he measured a thousand, and brought me through the waters; the waters *were* to the knees. Again he measured a thousand, and brought me through; the waters *were* to the loins. Afterward he measured a thousand; *and it was* river that I could not pass over: for the waters were risen, waters to swim in, a river that could not be passed over."

Our desire should be to take the Spirit of God we receive in this house, outside the four walls. The furthest we go from His House we should be deeper still, and not grow weaker. The distance of the

4,000 cubits measured here relates to just more than a mile. The depth God wants to take us to, *is exhilarating!* May we forge out and into the deep for the things of God!

I Corinthians 2:9-10 " But as it is written, Eye hath not seen, nor ear heard, neither have entered into the heart of man, the things which God hath prepared for them that love him. But God hath revealed *them* unto us by His Spirit: for the Spirit searcheth all things, yea, the *deep things* of God."

Come, Holy Spirit, I need Thee Come, Sweet Spirit, I pray

Come in Thy strength and Thy power

Come in Thine own special way.   (song)

THY ROD AND THY STAFF

Earlier this week as I awoke I told the Lord, "Your Word fascinates me!" I had been meditating on the Psalm, "Thy Word is a lamp unto my feet and a light unto my path." He led me to the beloved Psalm 23:4c "Thy rod and Thy staff they comfort me." I thought the rod was a term of the word staff and was fascinated they were separate in one sentence.

Isaiah 11:1 "And there shall come forth a rod out of the stem of *Jesse,* and a Branch shall grow out of his roots." *announcing our Messiah.*

Exodus 4:17 "And thou shalt *take this rod in thine hand,* wherewith thou shalt do *signs."*

Before the tenth Plague, the Lord God gave directions how to prepare and to be prepared for the Passover meal:

Exodus 12:11 "And thus shall ye eat it, with your loins girded, your shoes on your feet, and *your staff in your hand* and ye shall eat it in haste: it is the Lord's Passover."

In comparison, the New Testament declares: Ephesians 6:14-17 "... having your *loins girt about with truth...your feet shod with the preparation of the gospel of peace...taking the shield of faith... and the sword* of the Spirit which is the Word of God."

A staff was a treasure passed down the family line, for it had inscribed upon it the names of their descendants. Imagine the *staff* our Heavenly Father has of His own!

Deuteronomy 23:20 "...the Lord thy God may *bless* thee in all that thou settest thine hand to do."

Exodus 4:2 "...what is *that* in thine hand?"

WHAT SHALL I PUT ON?

"What shall I put on," I said as I stood before my closet on Mother's Day."

Luke 12:22 "And He said unto His disciples, therefore I say unto you, take no thought for your life, what ye shall eat; neither for the body, what ye shall put on."

As believers, we are admonished in Paul's writing in Ephesians 6:11 to "put on the whole armour of God, that ye may be able to stand against the wiles of the devil." The armour included, your loins girt about with truth, having on the breastplate of righteousness, your feet shod with the preparation of the gospel of peace, the shield of faith, the helmet of salvation, and the sword of the Spirit."

Romans 13:12 "Let us therefore cast off the works of darkness, and let us put on the armour of light."

As Jesus told of the parable of the prodigal son returning to his father's house...

Luke 15:20 "And he arose, and came to his father. But when he was a great way off, his father saw him, and had compassion, *and ran,* and fell on his neck, and kissed him."

The confession and repentance in verse 21:

"And the son said unto him, father, I have sinned against heaven, and in thy sight, and am no more worthy to be called thy son."

The reconciliation and rejoicing in verses 22 and 23:

"But the father said to his servants, bring forth the best robe, and *put it on him; and put a ring on his hand, and shoes on his feet.* And bring hither the fatted calf, and kill it; and let us eat and be merry."

Colossians 3:10,12-16 "...And have *put on the new man,* which is renewed in knowledge after the image of Him who created him. *Put on* therefore, as the elect of God, holy and beloved, *bowels of mercies, kindness, humbleness of mind, meekness, long suffering; forbearing one another, and forgiving one another.* And above all these things *put on charity,* which is the bond of perfectness. And let the peace of God rule in your hearts, to the which also ye are called in one body; and *be ye thankful* Let the word of Christ dwell in you richly in all wisdom; teaching and admonishing one another in psalms and hymns and spiritual songs, singing with grace in your hearts to the Lord."

Put on the garment of praise For the Spirit of heaviness Lift up your voice to God Praying in the Spirit

And with understanding, 0, magnify the Lord. (song)

FOR ME TO LIVE IS CHRIST

Matthew 16:15-18 "But whom say ye that I am?

And Simon Peter answered and said, Thou art the Christ, the Son of the Living God. And Jesus answered and said unto him, blessed art thou Simon Barjona: for flesh and blood hath not revealed it unto thee, but My Father which *is* in heaven. And I say also unto thee, that thou art Peter and upon this rock I will build My church and the gates of hell shall not prevail against it."

Six days later, Jesus took Peter, James, and John to a high mountain:

Matthew 17:2-4 "And was transfigured before them: and His face did shine as the sun, and His raiment was as white as the light. And behold, there appeared unto them Moses and Eli'as talking with Him. Then answered Peter and said unto Jesus, Lord, it *is* good for us to be here: if Thou wilt, let us make here three tabernacles: one for Thee, and one for Moses, and one for EIi'as."

Days later, when Jesus was led away to be tried by Caiaphas the high priest, where they had spit in Jesus' face and buffeted Him, Peter followed afar off to watch. Three times he denied the

Lord by saying, "I do not know the man." Matthew 26:69-75

After the Resurrection of Jesus, He had shown Himself to His disciples. It was this third time when Jesus said: John 21:15-17 "Simon Peter, lovest Thou Me more than these? He saith unto Him, yea, Lord; Thou knowest that I love Thee. He saith unto him, feed My lambs. Again He said, lovest thou Me? Peter said, yea, Lord; Thou *knowest* that I love Thee. He saith unto him, feed My sheep. He saith unto him the third time, lovest thou Me? Peter was grieved because He said unto him the third time and said, Lord, Thou *knowest that I love Thee.* Jesus saith unto him, feed My sheep."

The first two questions, agape love was used, a supreme love. Peter answered them with a 'fond of type of love. The third question, Jesus used the 'fond of type of love which deeply humbled Peter.

Peter chose to live for Christ and being part of experiencing the impartment of the Holy Ghost in the Upper Room, he began preaching to the people and many were converted that day.

Acts 2:41 Three thousand conversions and

Acts 4:4 Five thousand more

May we choose to live for Christ, so much, that we *never* would deny Him!

God's Covenant

God chose unto Himself a nation, Israel. He intended His love of Israel to hold fast to passionate degrees of His mighty acts on their behalf. This type of love guaranteed Israel would have this unique relationship with God forever.

Deuteronomy 7:8-9 "Because the Lord loved you and because He would keep the oath which He had sworn unto your fathers, hath the Lord brought you out with a mighty hand, and redeemed you out of the house of bondmen. Know therefore that the Lord thy God, He is God, the faithful God, which keepeth covenant and mercy with them that love Him and keep His commandments to a thousand generations."

Again, in 1967 through the Six Day War, God brought Israel out with His mighty hand.

Deuteronomy 7:18 ",..but shalt *well remember what the Lord thy God did.*"

When we hear reports of turmoil arising in the Middle East, pray and let God be God.

Philippians 4:8,7 "Finally, brethren, whatsoever things are *true,* whatsoever things are *honest,* whatsoever things are *just,* whatsoever things are *pure,* whatsoever things are *lovely,* whatsoever things are *of good report* if there be any virtue, and if there be any praise, think on these things. And *the peace of God,* which passeth all understanding, *shall keep your hearts and minds through Jesus Christ."*

comment added to, *Gods Covenant :*

My husband asked me to put this devotion on Facebook, which was nothing new for him to do. I was so surprised to see that he had shared it with Benjamin Netanyahu, Prime Minister to Israel. He commented, "Thank you good people. God bless them all!"

I believe he blessed all of America with his words - and I'm humbled to have a Jewish blessing spoken forth into our lives.

AMERICA PRAY

Today, Sept 28, 2012, is the onset of "If My People 2012, 40 Days of Prayer for America" leading up to Election Day. *As* we go to the Lord in prayer, lifting our nation up before the Lord, remember what miracle God wrought for Israel in their first war:

Exodus 17:9-15 " And Moses said unto Joshua, Choose us out men, and go out, fight with Amalek: tomorrow I will stand on the top of the hill with the *rod of God in mine hand* So Joshua did as Moses had said to him, and fought with Amalek: and Moses, Aaron, and Hur went up to the top of the hill. And it came to pass, *when Moses held up his hand, that Israel prevailed.* and when he let down his hand, Amalek prevailed. But Moses' hands *were* heavy; and they took a stone, and put *it* under him, and he sat thereon; and Aaron and Hur stayed up his hands, the one on the one side, and the other on the other side; and his hands were steady until the going down of the sun. And Joshua discomfited Amalek and his people with the edge of the sword. And the LORD said unto Moses, Write this *for a* memorial in a book, and rehearse it in the ears of Joshua: for I will utterly put out the remembrance of Amalek from under heaven. And Moses built an altar, and called the name of it Jehovah-nissi:"

Jehovah-nissi means, the Lord our Banner; which is a covering. May God cover and preserve our nation - as we cover our nation in prayer.

THE LORD HATH BLESSED US

God's Word, the Bible is the Living Word and *life* to us. We can claim and stand on God's Word. We should prepare ourselves to think outside the box. Don't limit God to what you think He will do. Let's claim these verses for our nation.

Isaiah 61:9-11 "...all that see them shall acknowledge them, that they *are* the seed *which* the LORD hath blessed. I will greatly rejoice in the LORD, my soul shall be joyful in my God; for he hath clothed me with the garments of salvation, he hath covered me with the robe of righteous - *ness, as* a bridegroom decketh *himself* with ornaments, and as a bride adorneth *herself* with her jewels. For as the earth bringeth forth her bud, and as the garden causeth the things that are sown in it to spring forth; so the Lord GOD will cause *righteousness and praise to spring forth before all the nations*"

Isaiah 62:3 "Thou shalt also be a crown of glory in the hand of the LORD, and a royal diadem in the hand of thy God."

Therefore the redeemed of the Lord shall return;
and come with singing unto Zion
an everlasting joy shall be upon their heads
They shall obtain gladness and joy
and sorrow and mourning shall flee away.
(song)

Predestination "Choose your Destiny'

Romans 8:28-30 "And we know that all things work together for good to them that love God, to them who are the called according to His purpose. For whom He did foreknow, He also did predestinate to be conformed to the image of His Son. Moreover, whom He did predestinate, them He also called and justified and glorified."

God gives us the choice to accept or reject His Son. All who do accept, He has foreknown and predestinated to be conformed to the image of His Son. Those who reject Him, He has foreknown and predestinated to be consigned to His eternal wrath. This is the extent of foreknowledge and predestination.

Ephesians 1:4 "According as He hath *chosen us in Him before the foundation of the world,* that we should be holy and without blame before Him in love, according to the good pleasure of His will."

At *that moment in time -*

God hath *chosen* us, hath *loved us,* hath known all our choices - even after we chose Him and made ourselves mistakes - He hath loved *them* too and hath *blessed them!*

Oh, the *mercy and the love of* God that is *known and shown bountifully toward us!* Seek out and live your destiny!

HOPE IN GOD

Psalms 42:11b "...hope thou in God: for I shall yet praise Him, who is the health of my countenance, and my God."

Col. 1:27 " To whom God would make known what is the riches of the glory of this mystery among the gentiles; which is *Christ in you, the hope of glory."*

Saturday night I was preparing this devotion and Sunday morning our guest speaker resonated, *"Christ in you the hope of glory."* He asked us to place our hands on our spiritual womb and to repeatedly say, "my soul doth magnify the Lord, my soul doth magnify the Lord!" In the hope of producing good seed in our lives. He concluded by saying, "breathe the hope in this room!"

I Peter 3:15 "But sanctify the Lord God in your hearts: and be ready always to give an answer to every man that asketh you a reason of the *hope that is in you* with meekness and fear."

The last verse of the next chapter in Psalms 43:5 rings out again, "...hope thou in God: for I shall yet praise Him, who is the health of my countenance, and my God."

I want a Double Portion

In our world today, we look for things we can have doubled. From double coupons to double pay for working on a holiday. At church you might hear your minister speak forth a double blessing or say he is experiencing a double anointing. When someone might say "I want a double portion," we may think it would be mashed potatoes, ice cream or anything delicious. *As* for myself I like my coffee with double cream and double sugar.

Most Christians would relate it to the awesome passage in the Bible when Elisha received a double portion of the spirit of Elijah.

II Kings 2:9-14 "... Ask what I shall do for thee, before I be taken away from thee. And Elisha said, I pray thee, let a double portion of thy spirit be upon me. And he said, Thou hast asked a hard thing: *nevertheless,* if thou see me *when I* am taken from thee, it shall be so unto thee; but if not, it shall not be *so.*

And it came to pass, as they still went on, and talked, that, behold, *there appeared* a chariot of fire and horses of fire, and parted them both asunder; and Elijah went up by a whirlwind into heaven. And Elisha saw *it* and he cried, my father, my father, the chariot of Israel, and the horsemen thereof. And he saw him no more: and he took hold of his own clothes, and rent them in two pieces.

He took up also the mantle of Elijah that fell from him and went back, and stood by the bank of Jordan; and he took the mantle of Elijah that fell from him, and smote the waters, and said, Where is the LORD God of Elijah? And when he also had smitten the waters, they parted hither and thither: and Elisha went over."

There were 16 miracles of Elijah and 32 miracles of Elisha. We can live our life now, asking God for whatever double portion you would ask of Him. *A double portion of boldness is mine, what's yours?*

SALT AND LIGHT

We are to be Salt and Light to the world. This is our slogan at Southeastern University. *As* we begin the 40 Days of Prayer for America, the prayer guide says:

"America needs the church. Not as good-deed doers, but as those who give direction for the future and who preserve and protect in the present. We are to be Light, helping people and nations avoid the pitfalls of darkness. We are to be Salt, both as seasoning and protection for our society. Pray, asking the Lord God for the church to rise up with a strong prophetic voice for America."

Salt is important to God. God spoke to Moses out of the tabernacle of the congregation, on how to prepare, season and present their offerings up to God.

Leviticus 2:13 "And every oblation of thy meat offering shalt thou season with salt; neither shalt thou suffer the salt of the covenant of thy God to be lacking from thy meat offering: with *all thine offerings thou shalt offer salt.*"

Romans 12:1 b "...that ye present your bodies a *living sacrifice,* holy, *acceptable unto God,* which is your reasonable service."

To be acceptable to God we must be salt. After Jesus spake The Beatitudes, He said, "Ye are the salt of the earth... ye are the light of the world...let your light so shine before men, that they may see your good works and glorify your Father which is in heaven." Matt.5:13,14,16

As God would accept the burnt offerings when the aroma with salt came before Him, may God accept our offering as we *live Salt and Light before Him!*

UNTO ALL PLEASING

In our childhood, there are times we can remember when we pleased our parents. It might have been doing whatever they asked of us, or seeing their eye of approval when picking up a brother or sister who had fallen down. I remember my mother beside me as I did my homework, trying to do my best hand writing possible and *she* said "good work!" Well, I was her first born child, so I guess she would have loved anything I did.

Colossians 3:20 "Children, obey *your* parents in all things: for this is well pleasing unto the Lord."

Later in my life I wanted to please the Lord while pleasing my parents. I worked in the family business and felt God's smile on me every day I entered the citrus store. My family and I moved to Tennessee and were caregivers to elderly in a boarding home. My parents moved my grandmother to us and we took care of her also. In honoring her I pleased God.

Colossians 3:23 "And whatsoever ye do, do *it* heartily, as to the Lord, and not unto men;"

By faith we please God. Hebrews 11 is referred to as *the hall of faith.* It takes you down that great hall of time when men and women who feared God, served Him by faith.

Hebrews 11:5-6 " By faith Enoch was translated that he should not see death; and was not found, because God had translated him: for before his translation he had this testimony, that he *pleased God.* But without faith it is impossible to please Him: for he that cometh to God must believe that He is, and that He is a rewarder of them that diligently seek Him."

Paul said in I Thessalonians 4:1 " Furthermore then we beseech you, brethren, and exhort *you* by the Lord Jesus, that as ye have received of us how ye ought to walk and to *please God, so* ye would abound more and more."

Colossians 1:10 "That ye might walk worthy of the Lord *unto all pleasing,* being fruitful in every good work, and increasing in the knowledge of God."

Do you Know your Value?

The body is wonderfully made.

Psalms 139:14 "I will praise thee; for I am fearfully *and* wonderfully made:..." It consists of various chemicals iron, sugar, salt, carbon, iodine, phosphorus, lime, calcium and others - about .98 cents worth.

When God created us, He reached into Himself. We are unique in our own way and treasured by God. He celebrates when we seek Him.

Job 28:27 "Then did He see it, and declare it; he prepared it, yea, and searched it out." When we seek Him, we search, we declare it, then we will see! The next verse declares: Job28:28a "And unto man he said, Behold, the fear of the Lord, that *is* wisdom:"

Do you know your value? Someone may be impressed by something you've done and ask you, "do you know your value? An acronym I have come up with for "Value" is:

Vessel

Assesses

Life

Using

Earnest

To *assess* means to value, judge the worth. Earnest is the intent on one's purpose. So, value is judging the worth of your intentions and purpose.

James 5:16 "... The effectual fervent prayer of a righteous man availeth much." The value in this verse, when you act upon it, *makes you valuable to God.* Let the value of His 98 cent investment in you - pay off in "Big" dividends and seek to be rich toward God.

Luke 12:15 "... for a man's life consisteth not in the abundance of the things which he possesseth."

Luke 12:21 "So *is* he that layeth up treasure for himself, and is not rich toward God."

Thanks be to God

Recollections of our life as far as we can remember is of a blessed one. We are so blessed of God - our children have the kiss of God on them, as we *see* blessings upon them. Yet we yearn to see our own seek a life with Him.

Psalms 100:4-5 "Enter into His gates with thanksgiving, *and* into His courts with praise: be thankful unto Him, *and* bless His name. For the LORD *is good* His mercy *is* everlasting; and His truth *endureth* to all generations."

Psalms 103:17 "But the mercy of the LORD *is* from everlasting to everlasting upon them that fear Him, and his righteousness unto children's children;"

Psalms 104:24 "0 LORD, how manifold are thy works! In wisdom hast Thou made them all: the earth is full of Thy riches."

Psalms 104:31 "The glory of the LORD shall endure for ever: the LORD shall rejoice in His works."

Psalms 104:34 "My meditation of Him shall be sweet: I will be glad in the LORD."

Favor Brings Destiny

Two women were favored of God, It was God's plan to favor Esther for the preservation of the Jews.

Esther 2:15-17 "... And Esther obtained favour in the sight of all them that looked upon her. So Esther was taken unto King Ahasuerus into his house royal in the tenth month, which is the month Tebeth, in the seventh year of his reign. And the king loved Esther above all the women, and she obtained grace and favour in his sight more than all the virgins; so that he set the royal crown upon her head, and made her queen instead of Vashti."

Her uncle Mordecai spoke special words to her that would resonate down through time: "...who knoweth whether thou art come to the kingdom for *such* a time as this? "Esther 4:14

This would also hold true to the Son of God's Mother, Mary. The angel Gabriel was sent from God to bring the annunciation of *Jesus* to the Virgin Mary.

Luke 1:28,31-33 "...and said, Hail, *thou that art* highly favoured, the Lord *is* with thee: blessed *art* thou among women."

"And, behold, thou shalt conceive in thy womb, and bring forth a son, and shalt call his name JESUS. He shall be great, and shall be called the Son of the Highest:

A Modern Day Bible Story

History has a way of repeating itself. We find it fascinating if its take is from the 'lawful' good side. This is a modern day Bible story come to life.

My pastors were vacationing in Israel and heard this while they were there. Israeli Defense Forces (IDF) were on a mountain and became trapped when the enemy surrounded the mountain at its base. Israel knew by morning they would come against them. Israeli's Defense Forces devised a strategy, knowing or unknowing this same strategy had been used before. At 3am in the morning IDF positioned vehicles half way down the mountain, facing the enemy. On cue, all the headlights were turned on and they blew all the horns to make noise - which startled the enemy and they scattered away for fear.

The mirrored Bible story is Gideon and his 300 men. They were on mount Gilead.

Judges 7:9,12 "And it came to pass the same night, that the LORD said unto him, Arise, get thee down unto the host; for I have delivered it into thine hand. And the Midianites and the Amalekites and all the children of the east lay along in the valley like grasshoppers for multitude; and their camels *were* without number, as the sand by the sea side for multitude."

Judges 7:19-21 " So Gideon, and the hundred men that *were* with him, came unto the outside of the camp in the beginning of the middle watch; and they had but newly set the watch: and they blew the trumpets, and brake the pitchers that *were* in their hands. And the three companies blew the trumpets, and brake the pitchers, and held the lamps in their left hands, and the trumpets in their right hands to blow *withal:* and they cried, *The sword of the LORD, and of Gideon.* And they stood every man in his place round about the camp: and all the host ran, and cried, and fled."

2013 Magnify Thee

Christmas was a blessed time in many ways. In my family, God showed up and preserved life. My niece, Christina has a heart for God, she helps her community through her thrift store business and sings like an angel unto the Lord. The day after Christmas she went into her bank and was the only customer there. Two bank robbers began a robbery and held an assault rifle to her. They told her they would kill her. She managed to go sit in a chair and pray. Being terrorized and emotionally distraught she prayed mostly for her son and family, thinking she may not be coming out of the bank alive. God showed up and answered her prayers. The robbers got away with 20,000 dollars; as only one policeman arrived at the scene.

1 Peter 4:19 " Wherefore let them that suffer according to the will of God commit the keeping of their souls *to Him* in well doing, as unto a faithful Creator."

Joshua 3:7 "And the LORD said unto Joshua, This day will I begin to magnify thee in the sight of all Israel, that they may know that, as I was with Moses, *so* I will be with thee."

I told my niece, "our family knows now that our God is more than awesome. You are not a completed work YET, He has more in store for you to touch, bless and be a part of His plan - you are His good pleasure!!

As we begin this New Year of 2013, know that we are not a completed work YET also. God has more in store for us. May we seek to be His good pleasure and say, "This day will I begin to MAGNIFY THEE!"

BE A KEEPER

When my son and his wife suffered through the passing of their beloved dog, I wrote them a tribute. This portion of it was the beginning of the idea of this devotion: "The day you both said your wedding vows, to have and to hold and to <u>keep,</u>' you also committed to giving Leo a life of happiness, together." To <u>keep</u> oneself only unto the other - as long *as* they both shall live.

Genesis 2:15 "And the LORD God took the man, and put him into the Garden of Eden to dress it and to <u>keep</u> it."

After God formed every beast of the field, and fowl of the air, He "brought them unto Adam to see what he would call them: and whatsoever Adam called every living creature, that was the name thereof." Genesis 2:19

When Adam and Eve's sons, Cain and Able had their conflict which led to murder, "And the LORD said unto Cain, Where *is* Abel thy brother? And he said, I know not: *Am* I my brother's <u>keeper?"</u> Genesis 4:9

Our brothers and sisters who cross our paths each day, we should have a desire to *uphold them* if they have a need. *As* with Adam, *God brings them our way to see what we will do.*

Psalms 121:5 " The LORD is thy <u>keeper:...</u>"

Isaiah 26:3 "Thou wilt <u>keep</u> *him* in perfect peace, *whose* mind is stayed *on Thee:* because he trusteth in Thee."

2 Timothy 1:12 "...for I know whom I have believed, and am persuaded that he is able to <u>keep</u> that which I have committed unto Him against that day."

Philippians 4:7 "And the peace of God, which passeth all understanding, shall <u>keep</u> your hearts and minds through Christ Jesus."

More than someone exclaiming, "he's a keeper or *she's* a keeper" *may God exclaim in heaven, when we ascend* in being a **<u>Keeper</u> of <u>Souls!</u>**

VIGILANT VIRGINS AND DILIGENT MEN

The parable of the Ten Virgins being likened to the Kingdom of Heaven illustrates watchfulness in view of the Lord's coming. The five wise Virgins could be vigilant Virgins because to be *vigilant* you are watchful, alert and aware.

I Peter 5:8 "Be sober, be *vigilant,* because your adversary the devil, as a roaring lion, walketh about, seeking whom he may devour."

To be *diligent,* you perform with intense concentration, focus and responsible regard.

Joshua called the Rubenites, the Gadites and Manasseh together to speak favorable words and blessing over them for their obedience toward Moses and himself.

Joshua 22:5 "But take *diligent* heed to do the commandment and the law, which Moses the servant of the LORD charged you, to love the LORD your God, and to walk in all His ways..."

When they came to the borders of Jordan they built a great altar, not for burnt offering or sacrifice but for a memorial, a witness between them and the other tribes and the generations after them "... that we might do the service of the LORD..." Joshua *22:27*

In this story a civil war between the Israelites almost surfaced. But God preserved His people as one, together through the *diligence* of His blessed ones through Joshua.

May we always perform with our focus on God, our concentration on track, and let everything be done for the *glory of God.*

GAME PLAN: ESTABLISH A LEGACY OF FAITH

In years past, we've heard of a couple NFL coaches who had made an impact through their **stand up** faith. Tony Dungy who was our very own Buccaneers Coach in our lo-cal, made a difference to his team players; bringing his faith in God in action on the field. When he left the Bucs to lead the Indianapolis Colts, I *was* saddened, but elated when he brought his new team players through unimaginable adversity - he led the Colts to victory in Super Bowl XLI.

Tom Landry build a dynasty with the Dallas Cowboys. I remember hearing stories of his faith in God when I was in High School. He remained with the Cowboys until he retired. Through the years, some would move on and new incoming players would attain the notoriety of being a Dallas Cowboy!

In the Evangel's Super Bowl outreach Edition there are seven NFL athletes proclaiming their trust in Christ through their legacy of faith.

We, at Southeastern are Team United. We are *in* the game, not spectators. What position are you?

When you are challenged - meet it.

When you **see** opportunity - seize it... and run!

John 15:15 "...I have called you friends; for all things that I have heard of my Father I have made known unto you."

I make you full partners and My personal representative on earth. You are to represent Me and reproduce My works as I represent God and did His works. (notation)

Speak Forth Blessing

Remember WWJD, Got Jesus? Now the buzz around campus is, "What is in your hand?" It makes a person think about the gifting coming from our lives to touch others. The simplest form of touching lives could be as easy as speaking into another life, a blessing.

Many children today are shunned by other classmates for anything they see fit to ridicule. There is such a need for teachers to become a life changer to their students. Years later the students would remember back to the day their life took a change - when they were shunned by classmates, but their teachers made them *shine!* *Blessings* spoken into one's life *releases* God's favor and can have a huge impact. The Bible speaks of giving double honor in 1 Timothy 5:17 " Let the elders that rule well be counted worthy of double honour, especially they who labour in the word and doctrine."

Let's anticipate what God will do, when we give blessing over our children and nation.

THE STORY OF JESUS

When I was eight years old, my father wanted our family to go to churches and sing... in front of them. He played his guitar and we sang "I Love to Tell the Story" and "Christ's Way is my Way." My brother being only three would only say "too, too" at the end of the song.

> Christ's way is my way
>
> through weather fair or stormy
>
> others have served Him and found Him to be true
>
> Christ's way is my way
>
> and can be your way too.   Too, too!

This week I've been singing, "I Love to Tell the Story." I had enjoyed watching "The Bible" mini series on TV and upon its completion, found out there were many encounters in God's spiritual realm that occurred. The man that played the part of Jesus saw his whole life in a flashback in front of his eyes, while he was on the cross. The crucifixion was shot for three days and he said, it was really excruciating. (the word 'excruciating' means 'out of the cross') *A* huge wind suddenly kicked up on an otherwise still night when Jesus told Nicodemus. "the Holy Spirit is like the wind."

and an irreplaceable part of Jesus clothing floated away. Several days later, a young boy who had traveled quite a distance, returned it. The cast and crew "knew" they were working on a very special production.

"I have glorified Thee on the earth: I have finished the work which thou gavest Me to do. And now, 0 Father, glorify Thou Me with Thine own self with the glory which I had with Thee before the world was. I have manifested Thy name unto the men which Thou gavest Me out of the world: Thine they were, and Thou gavest them Me; and they have kept Thy word." John 17:4-6

"I pray for them: I pray not for the world, but for them which Thou hast given Me; for they are Thine." John 17:9

"And for their sakes I sanctify myself, that they also might be sanctified through the truth. Neither pray I for these alone, but for them also which shall believe on Me through their word; That they all may be one; as Thou, Father, *art* in Me, and I in Thee, that they also may be one in Us: that the world may believe that Thou hast sent Me."

John 17:19-21 "0 righteous Father, the world hath not known Thee: but I have known Thee, and these have known that Thou hast sent Me." John 17:25

May we be counted as them that know God and that *Jesus* "knew us" when He prayed for us.

I love to tell the story, of *unseen* things above,

of Jesus and His glory, of Jesus and His love.

I love to tell the story, for I know tis true,

it satisfies my longing, as nothing else can do.

I love to tell the Story, twill be my theme in glory,

to tell the Old, Old Story, of Jesus and His Love.

(song)

Look Unto His Face

To attempt to comprehend the in-numerable details when God created just the plants and animals, is unfathomable.

1Timothy 6:13 "...God who gives life to all things..."

I was holding my twelve day old grandson in my arms, looking intently into his face God has blessed us with. The television was on and I would momentarily *see* what *was* on and then look down into his beautiful face again. I found myself watching the program for a couple of minutes and when I looked down again I exclaimed, "his gaze never turned away. He was patiently waiting for me to again look into his eyes."

God spoke loud and clear in this. His gaze never turns from us. There is no shadow of turning. He is patiently waiting for us to *look unto His face* and to impress upon our minds a visual never to forget.

James 1:17 "Every good gift and every perfect gift is from above, and cometh down from the Father of lights, with whom is no variation, or shadow of turning."

When a woman has traumatic pain in child birth, the instant she is shown her life breathing baby, everything changes. The pain *seems* to not matter and the impression of that moment will last a lifetime.

Turn your eyes upon Jesus,

Look Full in His wonderful face,

and the things of earth will grow strangely dim,

in the light of His Glory and Grace.

(song)

What a wonderful fascination God reveals to His creation... Psalms 8:4 "What is man, that thou art mindful of him..."

when we look into the face of His gift *and* into the face of the GIFTER.

CLOSER THAN A BROTHER

We all desire to have friends. We, at most times treasure the brother or sister God has blessed us with, to grow up with in our family, and regard them more than friends. Proverbs 18:24 "... there is a friend *that* sticketh closer than a brother." In our friendships we get together to spend time together, to find out how they're doing and to be there for them, if they need you. We don't go to our friend only to ask them to do things for you.

With Jesus as your friend, He wants sweet fellowship with us and to feel our love for Him come through. He knows all we are going through, so we don't need to tell Him all our needs we want to have fixed. He says in Matthew 17:20 "If ye have faith as a grain of mustard seed, ye shall say unto this mountain, Remove hence to yonder place; and it shall remove; and nothing shall be impossible unto you."

When Jesus healed someone, He spoke to the sickness. Jesus healed a deaf-mute in Mark 7:34-35 "And looking up to heaven, he sighed, and saith unto him, Ephphatha, that is, 'Be opened.' And straightway his ears were opened, and the string of his tongue was loosed, and he spoke plain." He spoke to the winds and the sea and there was a great calm.

When you speak to your mountains, in the unseen realm, heaven goes to work, sending healing, breakthrough and victory.

John 14:12 "Verily, verily, I say unto you, He that believeth on me, the works that I do shall he do also; and greater *works* than these shall he do; because I go unto my Father."

May we strive to please our Father by being a friend to God and exercise our authority in the name of Jesus to speak forth the victory in people's lives.

A Cousins' Tribute

To be part of the family of the house of faith is God's plan for us. It is a special gift to be born in the family He chose us to be a part of. Elisabeth and Mary were cousins. Mary went to visit Elisabeth after an angel told her they both would give birth to a son. They too would be cousins.

Luke 1:41 "And it came to pass, that, when Elisabeth heard the salutation of Mary, the babe leaped in her womb; and Elisabeth was filled with the Holy Ghost:" And she told Mary, "... the babe leaped in my womb for joy." Luke1:44

Matthew 3:1-2,4-6 "In those days came John the Baptist, preaching in the wilderness of Judaea, and saying, Repent ye: for the kingdom of heaven is at hand. And the same John had his raiment of camel's hair, and a leathern girdle about his loins; and his meat was locusts and wild honey. Then went out to him Jerusalem, and all Judaea, and all the region round about Jordan, And *were* baptized of him in Jordan, confessing their sins."

Matthew 3:13-15 "Then cometh **Jesus** from Galilee to Jordan unto John, to be baptized of him. But John forbad Him, saying, I have need to be baptized of Thee, and comest Thou to me? And Jesus answering said unto him, Suffer *it to be so* now: for thus *it becometh us to fulfill all righteousness*..."

Jesus ministered to the multitudes back in Galilee and spoke of His testimony of John.

Matthew 11:7-11 "What went ye out into the wilderness to see? A reed shaken with the wind? But what went ye out for to *see? A* man clothed in soft raiment? Behold, they that wear soft *clothing* are in kings' houses. But what went ye out for to *see? A* prophet? yea, I say unto you, and *more than a prophet.* For this is *he,* of whom it is written, Behold, I send my messenger before Thy face, which shall prepare Thy way before Thee. Verily I say unto you, Among them that are born of women *there hath not risen a greater* than John the Baptist."

THE HEARTY OLIVE TREE

The Lord blessed me on my birthday, having my family with me around the table at Olive Garden, and prepared a way to write a devotion about it. I posted a picture of celebration on Facebook and received a wonderful comment, "Thy wife *shall be* as a fruitful vine by the sides of thine house: thy children like olive plants round about thy table." Psalms 128:3

The analogy is, the offspring would be plentiful, hearty, and dutifully responsive to the parents. Almost any olive tree has as many as ten or more new tree shoots growing up out of the root system around the tree.

In the Middle East these trees are plentiful around the countryside and are known for their tenacity. They grow in almost any condition of soil, and can thrive in great heat with little water and are virtually indestructible.

Genesis 8:11 "And the dove came in to him in the evening; and, lo, in her mouth *was an* olive leaf pluckt off: so Noah knew that the waters were abated from off the earth."

Whatever else succumbed the flood waters, the hearty olive tree was still alive! And today the olive branch serves as a universal emblem of peace.

Primarily, the olive tree symbolizes faithfulness and steadfastness.

Psalms 52:8 "But I *am* like a green olive tree in the house of God: I trust in the mercy of God for ever and ever."

In the first verse of Isaiah's prophecy of Christ's suffering:

"For he shall grow up before him as a tender plant, and as a root out of a dry ground:..." Isaiah 53:2

And as the day of the Lord cometh, in Zachariah's prophecy: "And his feet shall stand in that day upon the Mount of Olives,..."

Zachariah14:4

When the Lord returns in the second Advent.

THE LOVE OF GOD

Psalms 8:1,3-4 "0 Lord our Lord, how excellent is Thy name in all the earth! Who has set Thy glory above the heavens. When I consider Thy heavens, the work of Thy fingers, the moon and the stars, which Thou host ordained; what is man, that Thou art mindful of him? And the son of man, that thou visitest him?"

The fingers of God molded man into the form he was created. To contemplate that God would send His Son, in all His glory to take the form of His creation and dwell among man, is so intense.

Hebrews 2:17a "In all things it behoved him to be made like unto His brethren."

Hebrews 4:15b "...but was in all points tempted like as we are, yet without sin."

Hebrews 2:17b "... that he might be a merciful and faithful high priest in things pertaining to God, to make reconciliation for the sins of the people."

What *overwhelming love* this is, that God would do for His children.

"0 Lord our Lord, *how excellent* is Thy name in all the earth!"

ATTRIBUTES OF GOD

Eternal Eternity is God's signature. It's who He is.

Faithful God will always be there. What a comfort and encourage-ment to experience His faithfulness.

Good God abounds in Goodness and it is the drive behind His blessings.

Holy God is unique, set apart and unlike all others. Holiness not only emphatically separates God from sin but also emphasizes His righteousness to our sinfulness.

Immutable God lacks no ability. He controls, and is involved in everything.

Jealous God's zeal, passion and single mindedness to protect what belongs to Him.

Judge At the Cross, judgment and mercy met. Both were victorious.

Long-suffering God's long-suffering shows an infinite amount of power, mercy, patience, and love; all of which He has in abundance.

Omnipotent God is all powerful and is the source of His *own* power.

Omnipresent God is everywhere simultaneously and encompasses all space.

Omniscient God knows His creation completely. Ezekiel 37:3 "... 0 Lord GOD, thou knowest."

Righteous God is the ultimate standard for right and always does the right thing. His ways are right because He is right.

Sovereign God is supreme in power, rank, authority, virtues, decrees, work and is accountable to no one. He retains ultimate authority and will do what He pleases.

Truth Truth not only describes what God knows but also all He does and says including, creation, redemption, judgment, and each detail of every promise He makes.

Love God is the definition of love. Without Him love does not exist. God is LOVE. God's love is indestructible, undeserved, compassionate, constant, immeasurable, voluntary, and a *gift.*

Personal God desires for a personal relationship with the man and woman whom He created in His image. God has used nearly every relationship we know, to reveal

Himself to us: husband, father, mother, brother, lover, bridegroom, shepherd, creator and designer, King, provider, protector, teacher, counselor, friend, physician, master, servant and military commander.

Grace   Grace gives what is not deserved.

Merciful God's mercy is great. Mercy is interwoven with all other attributes of God. God's loving kindness initiates mercy. His Holiness insures its integrity. His truth guarantees its reliability. His power assures its duration. And His faithfulness demands its constancy. The results of God's Mercy are forgiveness, restoration, and praise on the part of those who experience it.

Drawing Near to God

Could anyone be privileged to know God as Moses knew Him? Exodus 33:11 "And the LORD spoke unto *Moses* face to face, as a man speaketh unto his friend." Is this attainable to anyone who desires it? We are at this moment, as close to God as we really *choose* to be.

How close to God do you desire to be? There are times when our soul truly longs for a closer relationship with God. But more often than not, we simply settle for a less demanding level of Christian living, and our longing for God waters down to wishful thinking.

Worship is the expression of our desire to know God and means, to come near. In Exodus 33:18 Moses expressed the compelling desire of his life, when he said, "I beseech Thee, shew me Thy glory." It was not enough to have God's Angel go with Israel into the Promised Land. Moses pleaded, "If thy presence go not *with me,* carry us not up hence." Exodus 33:15

The desire is what God uses to bring us to Himself.

Psalms 37:4 "Delight yourself also in the Lord, and He shall give you the desires of your heart."

In this picture of Cindy and I on her last day working with us, look into the door. *A* door within a door. God has opened unto us His Door. What shall we do with His wonderful gift? Do we access into His presence or do we ask of Him to send gifts from above?

MERCY - A TOUCH OF HEAVEN

"Blessed are the merciful, for they shall obtain mercy." Matthew 5:7

Mercy, an infinite and inexhaustible energy, and an attribute of God reveals His compassion. Nothing can change the tender mercies of our God. Forever His mercy stands - a boundless, overwhelming immensity of divine compassion. This divine touch of heaven is what the Spirit of God wants to give us. It is a remarkable thing that the merciful always obtain mercy.

His divine touch increases your thirst and appetite for greater things. Something within makes you press on until you are empty of everything else, so that you may be filled with what God is pressing in. God will not fail to fill us. No man can hunger and thirst after righteousness unless God has put the desire in him.

Within the Beatitudes, found in Matthew 5:3-10

Mercy is the only beatitude that is rewarded with the same; which means, when we show mercy the best we know how, God will adorn us with His mercy.

Lamentations 3:22-23 "It is of the LORD'S mercies that we are not consumed, because His compassions fail not. They are new every morning: *great is Thy faithfulness.*"

IMMEASURABLE GIFTS FROM GOD

Ephesians 3:17-19 " That Christ may dwell in your hearts by faith; that ye, being rooted and grounded in love, may be able to comprehend with all saints what *is* the breadth, and length, and depth, and height; And to know the love of Christ, which passeth knowledge, that ye might be filled with all the fullness of God."

To be *filled with God* is a good thing.

To be filled with the *fullness of God is* still greater.

To be filled with *all the fullness of God,* utterly bewilders the sense and confounds the understanding.

"God hath dealt to every man the *measure of faith."* Romans 12:3

But also grace, "To each one of us, *grace was given according to the measure* of Christ's gift." Ephesians 4:7

God's gift to man is the measure of *His* love. John 3:16 The *death of Christ* is the measure of *His* love.   Romans 5:5-10

And the *Holy Spirit* who transforms men and works in their lives, is the measure of the love of the *Spirit* to man.   John 16:7-15

The measure God gives is immeasurable to us.

Luke 6:38 *"Give,* and it shall be given unto you; good measure, pressed down, and shaken together, and running over, shall men give into your bosom. For with the same measure that ye mete withal it shall be measured *to you again."* This means double rewards for doing good.

Give... to you again.

THE TWELVE FOUNDATION STONES OF THE NEW JERUSALEM

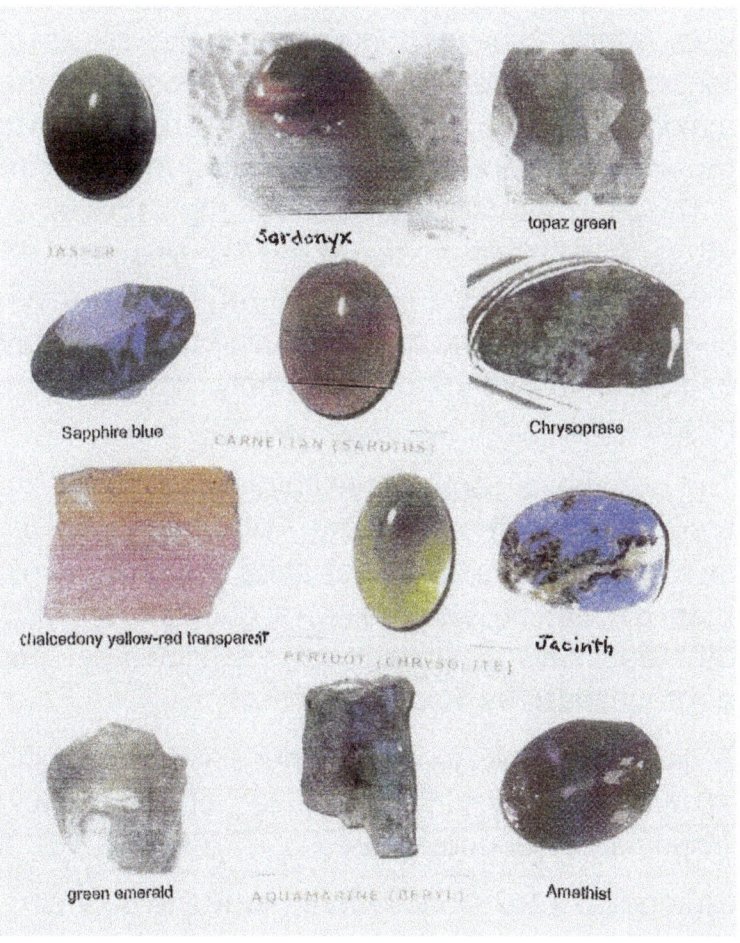

JASPER   Sardonyx   topaz green

Sapphire blue   CARNELIAN (SARDIUS)   Chrysoprase

chalcedony yellow-red transparent   PERIDOT (CHRYSOLITE)   Jacinth

green emerald   AQUAMARINE (BERYL)   Amethist

THE COLORS OF JESUS
in the Tabernacle and the New Jerusalem

Red, white, Blue and Purple are the colors of Jesus. God gave instructions to Moses in the making of the Tabernacle. There were five parts these colors were used: the hanging for the gate of the court yard that surrounded the Tabernacle, the curtains which made up the Tabernacle itself, the hanging for the door of the tent, the veil which divided between the holy place and the most holy and finally, the ephod, the holy garment the priest wore.

The purpose of using these colors is to glorify the Lord Jesus Christ! He came from heaven (blue) as the Son of God (purple) shed His Blood (red) that we can be washed from our sins and His Righteousness (white) is considered our righteousness by God the Father!

It is fascinating to know these colors will be within the precious stones of the New Jerusalem's foundations.

Revelation 21:2 "And I, John, saw the holy city, New Jerusalem, coming down out of Heaven from God, having been prepared as a bride, having been adorned for her husband."

Revelation 21:11 "Having the glory of God: and her light *was* like unto a stone most precious, even like a jasper stone, clear as crystal;"

Revelation 21:19-20 "And the foundation of the wall of the city having been adorned with every precious stone: The first foundation, jasper; the second, sapphire; the third, chalcedony; the fourth, emerald; the fifth, sardonyx; the sixth, sardius; the seventh, chrysolite; the eighth, beryl; the ninth, topaz; the tenth, chrysoprasus; the eleventh, hyacinth; the twelfth, amethyst."

Sardius a fiery *red* color stone; jasper, a crystal clear or sardonyx a reddish *white;* sapphire, a clear *blue;* and amethyst, a purple color stone make up the colors of Jesus. The other precious stones, with these, make up the colors in the most beautiful rainbow we could imagine. God's light passing through these many different colored stones will be breathtaking!

KEYS OF THE KINGDOM

The story of Esther is remarkable in many ways. Esther's Uncle Mordecai had told her, "and who knoweth whether thou art come to the kingdom for *such a time as this.*" Esther 4:14 This is something we treasure also to ourselves. We know God has a plan for our lives and we are in our time and place for a reason - to do God's will in *such a time as* we are living.

Jesus said in Matthew 16:19 "And I will give unto thee the keys of the kingdom of heaven: and whatsoever thou shalt bind on earth shall be bound in heaven: and whatsoever thou shalt loose on earth shall be loosed in heaven."

We can enjoy living in the kingdom realm, on a day to day basis - experiencing the blessings of God's kingdom on earth as it is in heaven.

Some keys are in knowing:

"...the joy of the Lord is your strength." Nehemiah 8:10

"Our soul waiteth for the Lord: He is our Help and our Shield." Psalms 33:20

"...greater is He that is in you, than he that is in the world." John 4:4

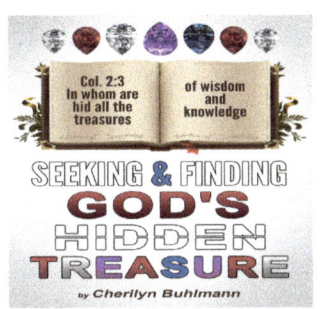

SEEKING & FINDING
GOD'S
HIDDEN
TREASURE
by Cherilyn Buhlmann

Proverbs 2:1-5 "My *son,* if thou wilt receive My words, and hide My commandments with thee; So that thou incline thine ear unto wisdom, *and* apply thine heart to understanding; Yea, if thou criest after knowledge, *and* liftest up thy voice for understanding; If thou seekest her as silver, and searchest for her as *for* hid treasures; Then shalt thou understand the fear of the LORD, and find the knowledge of God."

Proverbs 3:15 "She is more precious than rubies: and all the things thou canst desire are not to be compared unto her."

Romans 11:33 *"0* the depth of the riches both of the wisdom and knowledge of God! How unsearchable *are* His judgments, and *His ways past finding out!"*

Colossians 2:3 "In whom are hid all the treasures of wisdom and knowledge."

Proverbs 2:9 "Then shalt thou understand righteousness, and judgment, and equity; *yea,* every good path."

Proverbs 3:5-6 "Trust in the LORD with all thine heart; and lean not unto thine own understanding. In all thy ways acknowledge Him, and He shall direct thy paths."

Acknowledge is a form of knowledge. When we seek God, He reveals Himself in our lives. We involve Him in every part of our life; in turn, He orders our steps.

Psalms 37:23 "The steps of a *good* man are ordered by the LORD: and he delighteth in His way."

I encourage you to seek the things of God. Open your heart's door a crack and the Lord will excitedly come in and dine with you, and I guarantee, you will not ask Him to leave. His *hidden treasures,* you'll want to take a *lifetime to find!*

Make Me a Sanctuary

Exodus 25:8 "And let them make Me a sanctuary; that I may dwell among them."

God gives Moses the pattern of making the Tabernacle and all its furnishings. God said, "...even so shall ye make *it.*" Exodus 29:9

The Ark of the testimony and the Mercy Seat being the very first instructions. The Ark was approximately 45 inches in length, 27 inches in width and 27 inches in height. There is a crown in the center of the top so the Mercy Seat could be placed securely on it. The crown symbolizes and proclaims *Jesus* as KING of KINGS and LORD of LORDS. Christ's rightful position is forever secure. The Ten Commandments of stone, the golden pot of Manna and Aaron's Rod that budded were items preserved within the Ark. They are a statement that God's Law is to be fully kept, that Jesus is the Bread of Life and proclaims Jesus is the Resurrection and the Life.

The Mercy seat is exactly the same length and width as the Ark. God's eternal mercy is wide enough and long enough to cover everyone who abides in Christ. Of hammered work, two cherubim were made at the two ends of the Mercy Seat, of one piece. They were not fashioned by being poured into a mold, but were beaten out of one piece, signifying Christ's suffering.

Exodus 25:20 "And the cherubims shall stretch forth *their* wings on high, covering the mercy seat with their wings, and their faces *shall look* one to another; toward the Mercy Seat shall the faces of the cherubims be."

Exodus 25:22 "And *there* I will meet with thee, and *I will commune with thee* from above the Mercy Seat, from *between the two cherubims* which *are* upon the Ark of the testimony..."

We the church have been grafted in, and are heirs of the Kingdom. *Can* you imagine the pleasure the Godhead experiences when we take or lay hold of the things God has commanded of His own!

Let us come boldly before the Living Mercy seat in heaven just as we come boldly before the Throne of Grace when we pray. And let us make ourselves a living sanctuary for Him.

ABIDING IN CHRIST

When we abide in Christ, we make our abode with Him and He with us.

John 14:23 "If a man love Me, he will Keep My words: and My Father will love him, and we will come unto him, and *make our abode with him.*"

After John the Baptist baptized Jesus, he said, "...I saw the Spirit descending from heaven like a dove, and it abode upon him. *And* I knew Him not: but he that sent me to baptize with water, the same said unto me, Upon whom thou shalt *see* the Spirit descending, and *remaining* on Him, the same is He which baptizeth with the Holy Ghost. And I saw, and bare record that this *is* the Son of God." John 1:32-34

Not only John but whoever else was present saw this blessed manifestation come from heaven and make His abode with Jesus!

Psalms 91:1 "He that dwelleth in the secret place of the most High shall *abide* under the shadow of the Almighty." Dwelleth used here is, Hebrew - "yashah", which means: to sit down, to dwell, to *remain.*

1John 2:24 "... If that which ye have heard from the beginning shall *remain* in you, ye also shall continue in the Son, and in the Father."

Four things we can abide in are, the secret place (Ps.91:1) Christ (1Jn. 2:24) the love of Christ (Jn. 15:10) and one's own calling (1Cor.7:20) and above all, to remain in them.

Abiding in the Vine, abiding in the Vine.

Love, joy, health, peace He has made them mine.

I've got prosperity, power and victory

Abiding, abiding in the Vine.   (song)

Exercise your Faith

Driving by a fitness gym, the sign caught my attention, "exercise relieves stress." I began to ponder if we exercised our faith or exercised ourselves unto godliness, how much more than bodily *exercise* we could profit from.

Timothy 4:7-8 "...exercise thyself *rather* unto godliness. For bodily *exercise* profiteth little: but godliness is profitable unto all things, having promise of the life that now is, and of that which is to come."

In II Peter 1:5-8 Peter tells us there are eight virtues

that add up to security in Christ:

"Giving all diligence, add to your faith virtue,

and to virtue knowledge,

and to knowledge temperance,

and to temperance patience,

and to patience godliness,

and to godliness brotherly kindness,

and to brotherly kindness...charity.

For if these things be *in* you, *and abound,* they make you that ye shall neither be barren nor unfruitful in the knowledge of our Lord Jesus Christ."

Jesus had spoken, "0, ye of little faith" and "having faith as a grain of mustard seed." How much faith do we have?

If we reverse the eight virtues, *beginning* with Love because I Corinthians 13 says without charity, it will profit nothing. *Then add* brotherly kindness, godliness, patience, temperance, knowledge, virtue, then you'll *comprehend* your measure of faith... giving all diligence.

Two verses further in II Peter 1:10 "...give *diligence* to make your calling and election sure: for if ye do these things, ye shall never fall."

Personally this speaks volumes to me. *As* a Christian, God's love is within me. I look for opportunities to share His love and through brotherly kindness I can *see* God's love being edified. Living a life of godliness would automatically come forth and more of the virtues would follow. Then you will know in your knower... your *measure* of FAITH!

The Rebuilding of Jerusalem

Who did God choose to mandate the rebuilding of Jerusalem and the Jewish Temple? This man God chose, was prophesied 175 years before he was born, even foretelling his decree to liberate the Jews and to rebuild Jerusalem.

Isaiah 44:28 " That saith of Cyrus, he *is* my shepherd, and shall perform all my pleasure: even saying to Jerusalem, thou shalt be built; and to the temple, thy foundation shall be laid."

Isaiah 45:13 "I have raised him up in righteousness, and I will direct all his ways: he shall build my city..."

He is Cyrus, son of King Ahasuerus and Queen Esther! Before Queen Esther's knowledge that her life and all of Israel was at stake, her Uncle Mordecai told her "... and who knoweth whether thou art come to the kingdom for *such a time* as this?" Esther 4:14

For her contrite spirit and boldness given willingly, she was bestowed a blessing so precious - as soon as Israel was delivered, God would use her son in such a special way.

Ezra 1:2 " Thus saith Cyrus king of Persia, The LORD God of heaven hath given me all the kingdoms of the earth; and He hath charged me to build Him an house at Jerusalem, which is in Judah."

In the second year, the builders laid the foundation of the Temple of the Lord. There were hindrances which halted the work on the Temple. King Artaxerxes made them cease the work by force and power. After the Jews received a prophecy from Haggai and Zechariah, two men began to build the House of God and with them were the prophets of God helping them. This new work gave the enemies of Israel another occasion to deter them.

A letter was sent to King Darius which stated: "Now therefore, if *it seem* good to the king, let there be search made in the king's treasure house, which is there at Babylon, whether it be *so,* that a decree was made of Cyrus the King to build this House of God at Jerusalem, and let the king send his pleasure to us concerning this matter." Ezra 5:17

A search was made and there *was* found in the palace, a roll, and there *was* a record thus written.

Ezra 6:12 "...I, Darius have made a decree; let it be done with speed." The Temple was completed and dedicated. Feasts were celebrated with joy.

Ezra 6:22 "And kept the feast of unleavened bread seven days with joy: for the Lord had made them joyful, and turned the heart of the king of Assyria unto them, to strengthen their hands in the work of the House of God, the God of Israel."

Ezra *7:1* "Now after these things, in the reign of Artaxerxes King of Persia..." Ezra was favored.

Ezra 7:12 "In the King's words, *"and at such a time."*

A Way of Holiness

Is there a way of Holiness?

Luke 1:74-75 "...serving God in *holiness and* righteousness before Him, all the days of our life." This was a part of Zacharias' word from the Lord, when he prophesied after John the Baptist was born.

Paul speaks of a conditional promise to women in childbearing in I Timothy 2:15 "... if they continue in faith and charity and *holiness.*" And as they grow older: Titus 2:3 "...that they be in behavior as becometh *holiness.*"

When Christ comes for His Bride:

Ephesians 5:27 "That He might present it to Himself a glorious church, not having spot, or wrinkle, or any such thing; but that it should be *holy and* without blemish."

Holiness is God's true nature, is worship to God, praise to Him, separation to God, is of God's Throne and dwelling, is inscribed upon bells and pots, is of Christian living, of the eternal state and nature of believers in heaven, and is a literal highway that will lead up to the Temple of God in the Millennium.

Isaiah 35:8 "And an highway shall be there, and a way, and it shall be called <u>The way of Holiness.</u>" It will be the area from Egypt through Palestine to Assyria where people will travel on it, going up to Jerusalem to worship the Lord and keep the Feast of Tabernacles. Always remembering and giving honour to God for His provision and deliverance of His people when they had left Egypt.

Bloom Where you are Planted

Some inspirational plaques, you do not easily forget the message on it. One I found intriguing was, "Preach to the people - use words if you must." This reminds me of what Jesus said, "Ye shall know them by their fruits.... Every tree that bringeth not forth good fruit is hewn down, and cast into the fire. Wherefore by their fruits ye shall know them." Matthew 7:16, 19-20

The righteous " ...shall be like a tree planted by the rivers of water, that bringeth forth his fruit in his season; his leaf also shall not wither; and whatsoever he doeth shall prosper." Psalms 1:3

"That ye might walk worthy of the Lord unto all pleasing, being *fruitful* in every good work, and increasing in the knowledge of God;" Colossians 1:10

God's first command to Adam and Eve in Genesis 1:28 is "...Be *fruitful,* and multiply, ..."

We should obey this command, to *birth souls* into the Kingdom!

GLIMPSES OF HIS GLORY

Glimpses of his preincarnate glory which He had with the Father before the world was.

John 17:5 "And now, 0 Father, glorify Thou Me with Thine own self with the glory which I had with Thee before the world was."

Psalms 19:1 "The heavens declare the Glory of God and the firmament showeth His handiwork."

Every time the Bible says God created, we have another glimpse of Jesus preincarnate glory, being that the work was done by the Father through the Son. Christ was the chief worker or architect of the creation.

Moses was privileged to *see* the Lord's glory when he sought the Lord in saying, "...show me Thy glory." Ex. 33:18

"And the Lord said, Behold, there is a place by Me, and thou shalt stand upon a rock: And it shall come to pass, while My glory passeth by, that I will put thee in a cleft of the rock, and will cover thee with My hand while I pass by: And I will take away mine hand, and thou shalt see My back parts: but My face shall not be seen." Exodus 33:21-23

That is, cannot see My face in My usual glory and in the light that I dwell in, which no man has seen nor can see. Moses was then looking upon the visible face of God's Spirit body, as many others have. It was God in His infinite glory that Moses wanted to see. (notation)

Another glimpse of glory was when "...He took Peter, James and John up into a mountain to pray. *As* He prayed, His countenance was altered, and raiment was white and glistening. And behold, two men, Moses and Elijah who appeared in glory, spoke of His decease which He should accomplish at Jerusalem. The disciples were heavy with sleep and when they awoke, they saw His glory and the two men that were with Him." Luke 9:28-32

Glory will be personified on that day when the Lion of the tribe of Judah, the Root of David, hath prevailed to open the Book. "And lo, in the midst of the Throne, stood a Lamb as it had been slain..., and He came and took the Book out of the right hand of Him who sat upon the Throne. And when He had taken the Book, the four beasts and the twenty-four elders fell down before the Lamb, having every one of them harps and golden vials full of odours, which are the prayers of saints. And they sung a new song, saying,

Thou art worthy to take the Book and to open the seals thereof: for Thou wast slain, and hast redeemed us to God by Thy blood out of every kindred, and tongue, and people, and nation. And hast made us unto our God Kings and priests: and we shall reign on the earth.

And I beheld and heard the voice of many angels round about the Throne and the beasts and the elders: and the number of them was ten thousand times ten thousand, and thousands of thousands; saying with a loud voice,

> Worthy is the Lamb that was slain
>
> to receive *power,* and *riches,* and
>
> *wisdom,* and *strength,* and *honour,*
>
> and *glory,* and *blessing."*   Revelation 5:6-12

CPSIA information can be obtained
at www.ICGtesting.com
Printed in the USA
BVHW020947011119
562695BV00012B/78/P